IMAGES
of England
AROUND STANSTED
MOUNTFITCHET

Mum + Dad

With lots of love + Best Wishes

Sara-Jane + John

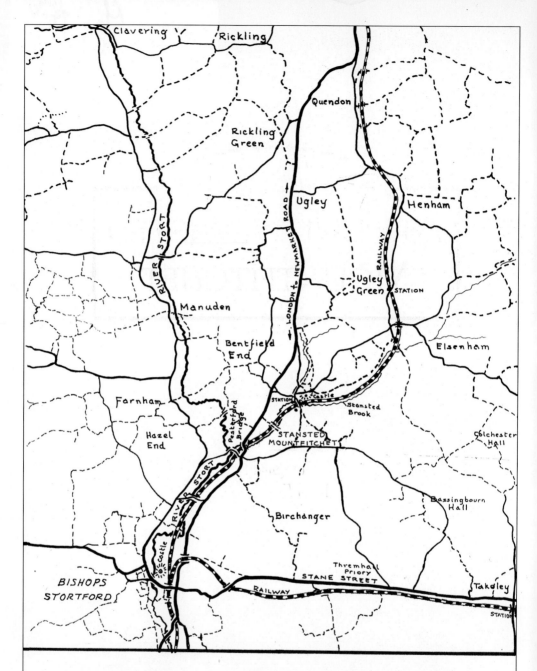

THIS MAP SHOWS THE AREA AROUND STANSTED MOUNTFITCHET
COVERED BY THE POSTCARDS AND PHOTOGRAPHS PORTRAYED
IN THIS BOOK. THE MAP IS BASED ON OLD MAPS AND DATA
FROM MID to LATE 19ᵗʰ CENTURY, IT IS NOT TO SCALE AND IS PRINTED
BY KIND PERMISSION OF HER MAJESTY'S STATIONERY OFFICE
© CROWN COPYRIGHT MC/98/211.   R.L.C. 1998.

IMAGES
of England

AROUND STANSTED MOUNTFITCHET

Compiled by
Paul Embleton

TEMPUS

Tempus Publishing Limited
The Mill, Brimscombe Port,
Stroud, Gloucestershire, GL5 2QG

ISBN 0 7524 1543 3

Typesetting and origination by
Tempus Publishing Limited
Printed in Great Britain by
Midway Clark Printing, Wiltshire

The ivy-clad stables for the Limes, shown on the extreme right of this 1916 view with the eighteenth-century windmill in the background and Crown Cottage to the left. In his reminiscences for the Local History Society, William Bunting recalled that his aunt liked to pose with her children for cards taken by their photographer. Judging from the frequency with which this same group appears in postcards of the village it is likely that this is them.

Contents

Acknowledgements   6

Introduction   7

1. Stansted Mountfitchet   9

2. Stoney Common and Birchanger   61

3. Bentfield End   69

4. Farnham, Hazel End and Manuden   75

5. Rickling Green and Quendon   81

6. Ugley and Ugley Green   89

7. Elsenham and Henham   97

8. Around Stansted Airport   107

9. Sports, Leisure and Local Organizations   119

Acknowledgements

I have been collecting picture postcards for twenty-five years and those of Stansted Mountfitchet since moving to the village some sixteen years ago. It is only in the past three or four years, since I started to talk to local societies about the history and development of the picture postcard, that I have collected cards from the surrounding area. Thus some villages covered in this book are under-represented in terms of the postcards produced over the last 100 years.

I have received much help from members of the Stansted Mountfitchet Local History Society and in particular I should like to thank the following:-

Ken and Janice McDonald for allowing me unfettered use of the Society's library; Jean McBride for lending family photographs; Margaret Silvester for allowing me to use photographs and quotations from her book on Rochford's nurseries; and Ralph Phillips for allowing me to reproduce a photograph and to quote from his booklet on Stansted's railway station. I have made use of recollections of Stansted residents who were interviewed by the Society some years ago, and also those residents of Ugley whose memories were published in *The Ugley Book*. I have not attributed names to memories except where I have had the approval of the person concerned. I thank the BAA for allowing reproduction of a photo from their celebratory booklet on the Airport.

I am very grateful to Bob Clarke for putting his drafting skills to such good use in producing a map to assist the reader to understand the topography of the area. I am also indebted to Peter Sanders for producing a very readable and informative introduction which sets the area into a historical context. Thanks are also due to Gordon Barker for assisting me with the captions for the Elsenham and Henham cards. My especial thanks go to Peter Brown whose enthusiasm and support carried me through those times when I thought this book would never make it to the publishers. His encyclopaedic knowledge of Stansted shows clearly in the captions which, without his input, would have been much less informative. I also thank him for the loan of a number of photographs.

Last, but by no means least, I must thank my wife Sandra, who for twenty-five years has patiently waited whilst I have taken any and every opportunity to browse dealers' stocks of cards looking for additions to my collection.

Introduction

The villages presented in this book lie close to Essex's western boundary and to the Hertfordshire town of Bishop's Stortford. For many villagers Stortford, as they call it, is their main shopping centre, and for centuries it has been their market town, the hub of the local economy. Others go northwards to Saffron Walden whose name derives in part from the saffron crocus on which its prosperity was once based. Less than half the size of Bishop's Stortford, it is one of the prettiest market towns in the county.

In 1888 there were plans to transfer five of these villages (Elsenham, Farnham, Manuden, Stansted and Ugley) from Essex to Hertfordshire, but this met with fierce local opposition and the plan had to be dropped. One villager pointed out that they had been part of Essex since the days of Alfred the Great and they did not want to be separated from their 'dear old county'.

These parishes are all rich farming land. In the past the agriculture was mixed, but in recent years more and more land has been turned over to arable farming. The river Stort, no more than a small stream at this stage, runs through the centre of the area from north to south. The countryside is gently rolling, and parts of the Stort Valley have been designated as a Special Landscape Area.

There is no good local stone for building and so the villages are rich in timber-framed houses, often with the pargetting (or decorated plaster-work) that is so typical of this part of Essex. The local clay has provided the warm brick and the peg-tile roofs which are such a feature of the area. It was only after the canal reached Bishop's Stortford in 1769 that slate began to be used in any quantity.

For some of the most picturesque cottage scenes in the country, the visitor is spoilt for choice. The village street in Manuden stands out, also Tye Green in Elsenham and Farnham Green and Hazel End in Farnham. Several of the churches, though heavily restored in the Victorian period, still add their own distinctive beauty, and huge timber-framed barns stand alongside the farmhouses.

The villages all seem to have been Anglo-Saxon settlements. Certainly they all have Anglo-Saxon names. Inevitably the name that has given rise to the greatest interest is Ugley, which has nothing to do with ugliness of appearance – far from it in fact – but is derived from Ugga's Ley, or a clearing in the wood belonging to Ugga. In earlier times genteel villagers tried to change the name to Oakley – fortunately without success.

When the Normans came, their most important centre in this area was Stansted, where Robert Gernon, one of the greatest landowners under William the Conqueror, established his headquarters at Stansted Castle. His estate was passed on to the Montfichets, who gave their name to the village, Stansted Mountfitchet, and who were among those who led the opposition to King John. They owned the land at Runnymede, where Magna Carta was signed, which is why the effigy of a knight and the words Magna Carta appear on the signs as you enter the village. It was at the time of the barons' wars with King John that their castle was destroyed. With the demise of the Montfichets, Stansted lost its pre-eminence, but it is still by far the largest of the villages covered in this book. The modern replica of its castle is now a tourist attraction, and its old church of St Mary, on the outskirts of the village, still has many Norman features.

The area has a strong Nonconformist tradition, going back to John Bagley, the vicar of Manuden, who was burnt at the stake in 1430 as a follower of John Wycliffe. It has strong sporting traditions too, and the cricket ground at Rickling is well known throughout the county. It has been the home of families and individuals who have made their mark in the country as a whole, like the Montfichets at Stansted, the Gilbeys, the wine merchants, who were based for some time at Elsenham Hall – and even Sir John Waad at Manuden, who as Lieutenant of the Tower of London had custody of Sir Walter Raleigh: 'that beast Waad,' Raleigh called him.

It has always been an important area for communications. The old Roman road of Stane Street, running between Colchester and St Albans, formed part of Takeley's southern boundary, roughly where the A120 runs today. The traffic of course was much less than today's, but even so in 1350 the canons of Thremhall Priory, just north of the road, were complaining that so many travellers came to them for hospitality.

Later, in the seventeenth century, the Great Newmarket Road, formerly the A11 and now the B1383, was built and improved so that King Charles II could travel quickly between his palaces (and his mistresses) in London and his stables (and his horses) at Newmarket. This became one of the busiest roads in the country, and the diarist Parson Woodforde described it as 'the best of roads' he had ever travelled. This was a great period for coaching, and to this day the road is lined with the inns which once catered for the coaching traffic. The milestones erected in 1747 by the Highway Trust that was responsible for the road can still be seen. The Highway Trust, the inns and the coaching trade flourished until 1845, when the first train ran through from Bishop's Stortford to Cambridge. Within a week 500 horses which had been used in the coaching trade were sold off at Cambridge. The Trust's staff, from Sir James MacAdam downwards, had to take a cut of fifty per cent in their wages. Road traffic did not recover until the coming of the motor car.

The railway, which was run by the Eastern Counties Railway Company (and later by the Great Eastern Railway) had stops at Stansted and Elsenham, but served the entire area. Because of the agricultural depression, the population in most of the villages declined in the latter part of the nineteenth century but, mainly because of the railway, the population of Stansted increased rapidly at that time. Today the frequent service to Liverpool Street (and the proximity of the M11) makes the villages popular with commuters. The increase in motor traffic led to problems of congestion, particularly in Stansted, and it was only with the opening of the M11 in 1979 that the pressure was relieved.

However, the most important development in communications has been the development of Stansted Airport. In 1942 a United States Air Force base was established in Stansted, and the new airfield was used by American bombers for their raids over Germany and the occupied territories. In 1966 this came under the control of the British Airports Authority, and passenger traffic began in earnest. Given that the airport's development is carefully limited and controlled, the area will surely continue to give much pleasure to resident and visitor alike.

Peter Sanders
Stansted Mountfitchet Local History Society

One

Stansted Mountfitchet

The pre-1918 'Golden Age' of postcard production and collecting was typified by the production of packets of six cards with a multi-view card displaying the set as in this 1911 card. The choice of view for such cards has varied little over the last ninety years with the principal streets and approach roads and the medieval parish church being preferred to the Victorian pile.

Because the village has developed around two north-south roads and the interconnection, this photographer's perception of there being a north and south division is a little unusual. This southern view from around 1910 shows the rail sidings in the foreground with Water Lane running parallel and the windmill with the house bordering the recreation ground running along the ridge.

The northern view shows the line of Chapel Hill from St John's church to the Congregational church with Water Lane at the left in the foreground and Woodfields and Sunnyside in the middle distance.

This 1912 view shows the London to Cambridge line and sidings which serviced the large maltings in the centre foreground. Also in view are the red-brick cottages of Water Lane.

Old Rustic Cottage, Bishops Stortford.

Entering Stansted from the south, the road crosses the railway at Pesterford Bridge, thought to be named after the adjacent Pest House. On the high ground above Forest Hall Road stands this delightful thatched house which so typified rural England that it was used by many national publishers with titles similar to this 1914 edition. Developments over the years means that it is now barely recognizable.

The road from Bishop's Stortford was the A11 trunk road to Norwich, now the B1383, with the Old Bell Inn just visible at the top of the rise. It is hard to believe that the road was ever so free of traffic as in this view from around 1907, although at this time residents complained of speeding traffic, particularly on Newmarket race days. Even after the construction of the M11, traffic continues to flow endlessly along this stretch.

Gypsy Lane/New Farm bridge crossing the River Stort at the point where it is joined by Stansted Brook. Apart from the fishing, the deeper stretches were popular with swimmers. This new brick bridge was constructed to allow better access to New Farm and provides an alternative route to Bishop's Stortford and Manuden.

This 1920s view conveys something of the rural nature of Lime Kiln Lane which meanders around the western outskirts of the village before dividing to Bentfield End, Hazel End and Manuden. The view is virtually unchanged today, although the thatched cottage now has a tiled roof.

As its name suggests, the lane served the lime kiln and pit which subsequently was used as a rubbish dump and is now green fields. This view dates from around 1916. An advertisement shows that in 1874 lime from this kiln cost 5d a bushel or just over $\frac{1}{2}$d per gallon.

The Limes is an imposing residence standing on a bank above the old A11 as it enters the village. At the time of this photograph (c. 1920) it may well have been occupied by the Gold family who were influential in village affairs. It borders the Stansted/Birchanger parish boundary.

Crown Cottage, Stansted.

Crown Cottage was originally the Rose and Crown commercial inn with a yard and stabling for eighteen horses. The cottage with the white boards is still instantly recognizable today.

Blythwood Dairy, *c.* 1905. This 'Most Modern Dairy' was opened with a golden key in 1892 by the Prince of Wales, under the watchful accompaniment of many members of the local nobility, family and friends, including the Gilbeys, Golds, Blyths and Lady (Daisy) Warwick. The building still stands as a private residence, though much altered over the years.

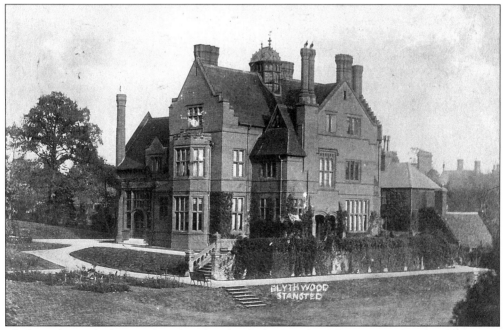

Blythwood was the home of Lord and Lady Blyth, friends of the Prince of Wales (later King Edward VII) and very much part of his social set. With Lady Warwick only a few miles away at Great Easton, this was a spot much favoured by the King.

COUNTRY HOUSE FIRE.

LORD BLYTH SAVED BY NEPHEW.

(FROM OUR SPECIAL CORRESPONDENT.)

BISHOP'S STORTFORD, AUG. 11.

Blythwood, the house of Lord Blyth, at Stansted, near Bishop's Stortford, Essex, was burnt down by fire early this morning. Only the outer walls are intact. The interior is completely gutted, and most of the furniture, pictures, and personal effects are destroyed. The house, an extensive building in red brick, was built in 1884.

Lord Blyth, his nephew and heir, Mr. Ian Blyth, and seven servants were asleep in the house, and were only aroused when it was well on fire. No lives were lost, but Lord Blyth and five female servants were rescued with considerable difficulty from the upper floors by means of ropes and ladders, after their escape by the only staircase had been cut off by the flames. Lord Blyth had his ankle twisted in the descent, and two of the servants were so injured that they had to be removed to Bishop's Stortford Hospital—the one suffering from burns and shock and the other from hurts suffered by a fall from a ladder.

The fire was discovered about 2 a.m. by the butler and footman, who slept in the basement. As the staircase was then a roaring mass of flames and smoke —as the butler described it—they were unable to get to the upper floors, but they succeeded in arousing the sleepers above by their shouts of " fire," and then ran to the outhouses for ladders. Lord Blyth, who is an invalid, needing a bath-chair to move about his house and grounds, could hardly have been got down from his bed room on the first floor by a ladder. Fortunately, Mr. Ian Blyth, who slept on the same floor, had a length of stout rope in his bed room, and, tying this round Lord Blyth, he succeeded in lowering him from the bed room window. As Lord Blyth was nearing the ground the rope became untied and slipped, and he fell some distance to the ground, injuring his ankle.

BUTLER'S RESOURCE.

Of the servants, the two in the greatest danger were Miss Hurrell, the housekeeper, and Mrs. Green, the cook, who both slept on the second floor. To reach their window, which was about 30ft. high, two ladders had to be tied together, and by this rickety appliance the butler, Albert Hacworth, helped to get them down. The housekeeper, who had to pass through the flames to join the cook, was badly burnt about the body. She was first brought out without any mishap. The cook fell from the ladder as she was half way down, but was saved from serious, if not fatal, injury by the butler, who, by seizing hold of her, stopped her from falling with all her weight to the ground. The three maidservants were afterwards brought out uninjured from a window on the first floor.

Before leaving the burning building, Green, the footman, telephoned for the police and fire brigade. Mr. Rupert Blyth (Lord Blyth's brother) and his wife, who were staying in a cottage in the grounds, and many of the villagers, as well as the police, were brought to the scene by the alarm. The three local fire brigades, Stansted, Bishop's Stortford, and Sawbridgeworth, arrived very promptly, and one of the brigades utilized an ornamental pond in the grounds, another drew from the main on the public road, and the third connected their hose-pipes with a running brook almost half a mile away.

The greatest praise is given to the butler. " What would have happened but for him is too terrible to think about," said Mrs. Rupert Blyth. " He was simply splendid. But for his discovery of the fire and his rescue work it is probable that everybody in the house would have been burnt to death." In reply to an inquiry as to the condition of Lord Blyth, she said he was as well as could be expected, having regard to the ordeal through which he had passed.

In 1926, Blythwood burnt down as recorded in this newspaper article.

Silver Street in 1911 shows a variety of shops including Tissiman & Sons, still well known today as a high class outfitters in neighbouring Bishop's Stortford. The soldier was almost certainly billeted at one of the Territorial military encampments. The Cock beer house sign is just visible on the left; its keeper at the time was Mr Conway.

A slightly later view, *c.* 1916, looking south in which the soldiers are again prominent. On the right the Windmill pub is selling Fordham's ales. The newspaper placard proclaims the loss of a British destroyer. Next door is Savage's the hairdressers and beyond that is Muffett's the fishmongers.

A 1920s view of Bunting's fancy goods shop, well remembered still by some of the older residents of Stansted. Further down, the antlers on the wall mark Chopping's the taxidermist. Other shops are Bloom the confectioner, Hawkins the bakers and Francis the watchmakers, while on the right the garage, one of several for such a small village, is probably Gray & Sons.

Adams the newsagent has replaced Miss Bunting and placards outside display stories such as 'Backs to the wall in Ethiopia' and 'Royalist America' by Eric Linklater. It is the *Daily Herald*'s 'That Wembley Penalty' which enables us to date this as May 1938, when Mutch's penalty gave Preston a 1-0 victory over Huddersfield.

By the 1960s most of the shops have become private homes, although A. Rose, confectioner, is still in evidence. This is now the longest surviving shop in the village. The Windmill is now selling Flowers ales whilst Deamer's newsagents has replaced H. Leach before it moved further along the Cambridge Road. Opposite is Player's boot and shoe repairer whose motto was 'Repairs left, repaired right'.

'Paringa Nursing Home' in Silver Street, c. 1926, now an antique shop. At a later date, an advertisement states that it offers 'Medical, Surgical, Maternity etc, every care and attention given, Nurses sent out for duty, day and night services. Apply sister in charge'.

Chapel Hill, connecting Cambridge Road (the old A11) and Lower Street, derived its name from the chapel which stood at the junction with Silver Street and Cambridge Road. It was built in 1492 but ceased to be used for religious purposes with the Dissolution of the Monasteries. It was in use as a blacksmith's shop when it was demolished in around 1870. Here demolition is under way.

A elegant cast-iron drinking fountain was erected on the site of the demolished chapel and was opened by Mr Gilbey on 1 May 1871, following which he took a good draught. It seems to have attracted the local livestock in this view postmarked 1906 but probably taken around 1902.

In this 1904 scene, Edward Cawle can be seen with his daughter Gladys, later Mrs Palmer. The clock to celebrate Queen Victoria's Diamond Jubilee was installed by the Stansted watch and clock maker J. Francis and was illuminated by gas light at night. Sadly it now only tells the right time twice a day.

THE FOUNTAIN & SILVER STREET, STANSTED.

In 1907, the distance to Cambridge has lengthened by a mile from the previous view though whether this was due to physical changes somewhere along the road or through re-measurement is uncertain. The ornate gas lamp is sadly no more.

The markings on the kerb used to assist motorists during the blackout dates this to the mid-1940s. The seat is still today a popular, and shady, resting place for villagers and cyclists alike.

The Essex county badge between the door and bay window of the building opposite the fountain marks this as the Stansted police station. Notices were displayed on the garage door. The milepost has by this time been relocated to the other side of the road. The site just to the right was redeveloped in the property boom of the 1980s to provide a grand office block which was never occupied and which is now to be converted to residential use.

This view from around 1906 looking south shows Chapel Cottage on the extreme left. It was later demolished to make way for further development in Clarence Road. Galloping Horse Villa in the middle distance was built by H. Thurston of the famous showground family and it was here that they stored and maintained their rides during the closed winter season.

By 1913, the villa had become the shop for Mathews & Kirk, motor garage and cycle agents.

This card from around 1909 captures a magnificent assembly of staff, pedal and motor cycles gathered in front of Mathews cycle store and Boyers motor garage in Cambridge Road. Above the door arch can be seen a galloping horse, whilst above the main arch are the 'hive' of industry, a lion guarding the 'horn' of plenty and the 'dove' of peace. While passing through Stansted, Charles G. Harper, the foremost topographical writer of his day, was less than complimentary about its architecture.

This scene from around 1915 is about as busy as Stansted ever got in those days. The Bell Inn had a garage with Jardine Engineering works alongside. It is probable that the people in the doorway were either the Archers or the Kemps who were landlords at this time. Next door is Mrs Kitson, the basket maker, who had the enviable telephone number Stansted 1. The shafts of the cart in the far distance are outside Bedlow's the wheelwrights.

In this 1920s view of Green's Garage, workmen pose beneath the archway leading through to their workshop beyond. This building is now the Co-op and it is presumed that the carvings of Galloping Horse Villa still lie beneath the façade.

A quiet 1960s view looking south shows that the garage, engineering works and tree are long gone. By this time the ubiquitous television aerial has begun to make an appearance.

Cambridge Road looking north in around 1930, showing Mayhew's garage and showrooms, with Mr Mayhew outside, referred to by the writer of the card as a new garage, with the Co-op next door. Petrol was dispensed from the arm straddling the pavement, a practice that has long since disappeared in all but a very few garages in Britain.

Cambridge Road, Stansted.

140328

This view from 1963 shows a large house, now demolished, on the corner of Croasdaile Road and the to be built Hargrave Close. On the right, the public footpath shows where a new access road Norman Way was built to old people's homes. Mr Norman was famous for his ginger beer which was sold in stone and glass containers which today are highly prized by collectors.

Three Colts, Stansted, Mountfitchet.

In this early 1970s view of the northern end of the village, the Three Colts can be seen with a private house just beyond, originally the Primitive Methodist chapel.

27

Mary MacArthur Holiday Home, Stansted. 1181.

Originally Hargrave House, and dating from around 1777, this was the home of the Pulteney family. It was converted into the Mary MacArthur holiday home for working women, being opened by Queen Mary on 31 March 1939. Residents recall lining the route and waving flags as the procession passed during a heavy thunderstorm. The ornate glass extension was known as the Winter garden or Sun Parlour. Today it is the Hargrave House Nursing Home.

The Large Lounge, Mary Macarthur Home, Stansted, Essex.

A view of the lounge of the house, which along with the dining room is one of the most common postcards of Stansted to be found. Nearly all have a message which relates to the good and substantial food and the nice walks in the vicinity. Wartime cards show that many women came for a rest from the heavily bombed suburbs of London, particularly the East End.

Green's Stores, *c.* 1910. The business was founded in 1687 and covered the reigns of fifteen sovereigns. The premises steadily expanded to accommodate the growing trade. Next door is Barclays Bank, the manager of the time being Mr Foster.

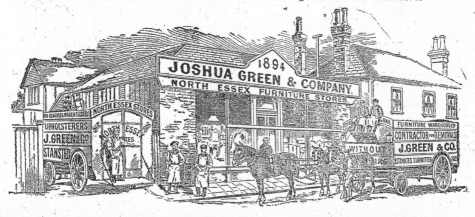

Green's Stores were regular advertisers in local newspapers. This is their removal advert from 1906.

In 1937 Green's Stores, with flag-bedecked frontage, full window dressing and shoppers, celebrated 250 years of service. Carved into stone above the door are the entwined initials JG between the dates 1687 and 1877 (the former date being when John Day opened his village store).

The staff of Green's Stores pose for the celebrations. Older residents recall that their customer service was second to none, with the highest standard of quality at lowest possible prices, and individual attention afforded to customers.

This specially designed 'Motor Travelling Shop De Luxe' was introduced by Green's Stores in around 1937 and faithfully served villages near and further afield with weekly necessities for many years. One resident of Manuden clearly remembers that, as a child, he queued for a can of paraffin dispensed from the tap at the bottom towards the front of the van.

J. GREEN & CO.

THE
NORTH ESSEX STORES,
STANSTED.

Agents for "NECTAR TEA."

The Novel Harvest Sale.

- - Held by - -

MESSRS. J. GREEN & CO.,

During the week ending
September 19th, 1908.

The Harvest Sale of J. Green & Co. in 1908.

The foot of Chapel Hill in the 1950s, showing in ascending sequence: the off-licence, Herrington's general store, Mr Barratt's Old Tudor tea shop, Wenn's the barbers and LMS Meat Co. On the left is the Kings Arms with the Barley Mow in the distance.

Another view of Chapel Hill where the rounded building was, until 1939, Brett's forge. Many older residents recall watching him at work and hearing his anvil ring. Later it became Mumford's the grocers and is now the local Spar shop.

The Bunting family is seen yet again in this 1916 view. To the right the entrance to Woodfield Terrace is just visible whilst further down an NCO with a swagger stick is taking a keen interest in proceedings. Prior to the road being covered with tarmac the buildings at the foot of the hill often were required to arrest the progress of runaway engines, carts, motors etc.

London Central Meat Company on Chapel Hill displaying a plentiful supply of meats. Mr Boothby proudly stands in the doorway with his assistants.

Half-way down Chapel Hill in this 1930s view stands Ecclestone's the chemist with large coloured glass jars and medicine bottles which drew admiring window gazers. Next door, the board advertises one of the early electrical firms in the village, T. Johnson & Sons.

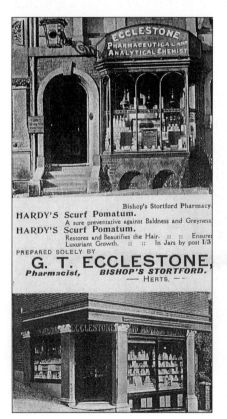

Ecclestone the chemist's advertisement in the trade directory. The Bishop's Stortford branch is shown above and the Stansted branch below.

Although posted in 1905, it is believed that this is an earlier photo of the post office, which was built in 1892. It is probable that this shows Mrs Holliday who was the postmistress at the time with the staff and telegraph boys. As late as 1927 the only public telephone box was located inside the post office which closed at 7.30 p.m. Apart from a new letter box, the exterior is much the same today.

Next door to the post office stands Central Hall, built in 1854, which over the years has had many uses: it has served as lecture and reading rooms, a literary institute, the Petty Sessional Court (with dungeon below) and a theatre, staging events by the Stansted Operatic Society, Scout gang shows etc. The poster advertises a public meeting to be addressed by two MPs, Buckmaster and Pease. It became a night club in the late 1970s before being converted into private flats.

One of many pubs in Stansted in 1915, the Barley Mow was converted to a private house in the 1960s. The writer states, 'This is one of the principal streets, about ten minutes' walk from the camp,' so he was clearly a soldier billeted nearby, perhaps on his way to the front. The high entrance steps were said to have been the downfall of many a patron at closing time.

This 1907 view shows the Congregational chapel of 1865 (now the United Reformed church) with the burial ground in front. The writer appears to be a servant at Stansted Hall and clearly had no love for it (or Stansted) as she closes: 'Hope to be in town [London] soon or anywhere rather than here'. In 1998, the church celebrated its tercentenary in Stansted.

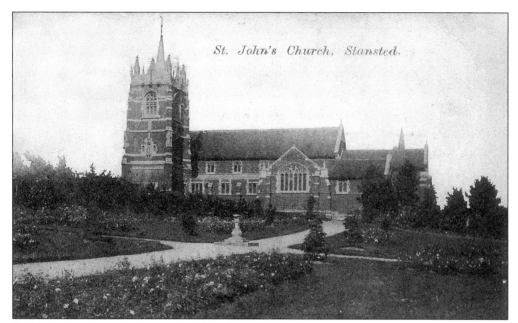

St. John's Church, Stansted.

St John's church was built in red brick and cream stone in 1889 as a chapel of ease, to the design of W.D. Caroe, the well known architect, then in the early stages of his career. Most of the funds were provided by the Pulteney family. This followed much debate as the existing parish church of St Mary was a mile from the village centre and in need of extensive and expensive repairs. In this 1905 view the church is still completely visible.

By 1923 the trees begin to obscure the church and the ornamental statue has been replaced by the war memorial with fifty-four names inscribed after the First World War. (Later another sixteen were added from the Second World War.) Recent research has shown that some names had little connection with the village, whilst others are missing who perhaps should be remembered. One or two names of residents of Stoney Common appear on this and the Birchanger war memorial, as they lived within Birchanger parish.

St. John's Road, Stansted.

By 1917, a small development of houses had been built more or less opposite the church in St John's Road. The lady is outside 'Inglenook' and the notice, which is difficult to decipher, appears to be advertising a dressmaker's. In the distance stands Little Flendish. Over the years all of the land to both sides has been developed, though until very recently the road was barely any better than eighty years ago.

View from S! John's Road, Stanstead.   92914

Looking east from St John's Road at a later date. The view is still unobstructed with the roof lines of Lower Street and Grove Hill visible in the distance. The Hawthorns on the ridge beyond dominates the skyline. Later this area became allotments before being developed. St Mary's School now occupies the site in the foreground.

Behind Chapel Hill lies the Recreation Ground with the Windmill beyond. The obelisk records the gift of the land to the village by the lord of the manor, William Fuller Maitland, in 1867. Village oral history records that children amused themselves by jumping over the shadow of the turning sails.

The Recreation Ground c. 1915. Children pose in their best dress under and around the gas lamp. If only we knew who they were!

Very few photographs seem to exist of the streets lying to the south of Chapel Hill. In this view of Sunnyside from around 1910, the red-brick houses and front gardens have a uniform look. In 1906 occupiers of these houses petitioned the Parish Council for street lighting and two lamps were fitted. The development of vacant ground to the right and the provision of parking places for the ubiquitous car have destroyed the uniformity of the view today.

Many soldiers were billeted in the village during the First World War and here they pose with Mrs Dixon and her family in Woodfields, another small street off Chapel Hill.

This card, also from the Dixon family album, shows a member of the family proudly displaying a brand new bicycle.

Stansted Mill and adjoining mill house, c. 1870. The windmill was built in 1787 by Joseph Linsell and his wife and ceased working in 1910. For the last seventy years of its working life it had been worked by Charles and Edward Hicks. It was purchased in 1887 by the first Baron Blyth of Stansted Mountfitchet.

Ye Olde Mill. Stansted. Essex.

The windmill has seen several alterations and modifications in its working life and now stands some 65ft high with a sail span of 66ft. In 1930, it was extensively repaired and restored by the second Lord Blyth who in 1935 conveyed it for the benefit of the inhabitants of Stansted. In 1952 it was scheduled as an Ancient Monument. From 1941 until around 1960 it was a unique headquarters for the village Scout troop.

In 1964 a volunteer force, now known as the Stansted Millers, raised funds and did much of the internal repair so that the mill could be re-opened, fully restored, in 1966. As the picture shows, small children are fascinated by it, and it is now a place to which many families come on open days.

The triumphal evergreen arch celebrates what was said to be the most important political gathering in the village in living memory. The Welcome banner was in bold Liberal colours upon a red background and marked the formal opening of the Liberal Club in Lower Street on 25 July 1888 by the Earl of Rosebery. The Liberal Club, as seen through the arch, had been built by a Stansted builder, Mr A. Sanders.

Lower Street in c. 1915. The Working Men's Club is prominent; the steward at the time was the quaintly named Z. Balaam. The decision to convert it from the Liberal Club was taken as early as 1892. Directly opposite is J. Wareing's tobacconist and the Queens Head (J. Burles, landlord). The photographer had no shortage of local children to pose in what looks like their Sunday best.

Lower Street in the late 1920s with Sanders and Forsdykes Stores showing windows full of goods and the hanging Gilbeys sign on what is now a private residence called Savages. On the road junction with Grove Hill stands Stansted Park Stores in front of which can be seen the Parish water hand-pump which was removed around 1932 after being dry for some time.

Sanders' General Store in Lower Street with a typical window display of the time. The premises are now divided into a hairdresser's, antique shop and florist's.

Sanders' advertisements from about the same period.

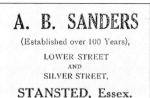

Local residents pose in this 1917 view of Lower Street with Brewery Cottages in the distance. The sun canopy is at Turner's grocery shop and perhaps it is Frederick Turner posed beneath it. The canopy of the Dog and Duck can just be seen in the distance on the right. This stretch of road was prone to flooding when the entrance to the barrel drain beneath became blocked with debris.

The shop premises of H. Whall, bootmaker and repairer, of Lower Street, who held the shop until about 1911. William Whall was recorded as being here from the early 1880s.

In 1911 the shop was taken over by W.C. Bunting & Son, florists and seedsmen. By the 1930s the business advertised itself as 'fruit merchants with all kinds of choice fruits and vegetables supplied at reasonable prices and garden seeds of reliable quality'. It continued trading into the 1980s.

A 1913 Christmas card showing Lower Street with Bunting's (seedsman and florist) and Mascall's the butcher next door.

Lower Street in the 1960s with the revamped Savages and Tudor House more or less as they look today. Other cottages have been converted into a newsagent's and a cobbler's while the owner of the bicycle is perhaps taking refreshment in the Queens Head.

On the junction of Lower Street and High Lane stood Tudor (or Brewery) Cottages dating from around 1600. In 1930 these were dismantled piece by piece and re-erected in Horsham, though some claimed they went to America. Efforts to trace the buildings have proved unsuccessful. Proposals and fund raising for a Village Hall on the site never got beyond the planning stage and eventually a private house was erected on it.

Lower Street in the 1950s, looking towards the Kings Arms.

A parade of floats in Lower Street for King George V's Silver Jubilee celebrations in 1935.

Mr Frederick Palmer with the float he dressed, outside Croft House stables prior to the parade.

High Lane, Stansted, Essex.

The tree-lined High Lane, the main road into the lower part of the village from the old A11, in 1957.

GROVE HILL, STANSTED

Grove Hill looking towards St John's church, c. 1910. In recent times traffic lights have been needed to control the traffic passing by the cottages just around the narrow bend.

Station Road in 1911 was mostly occupied by business premises or shops. The iron water trough can be seen just beyond the gas lamps, each of which cost £2 12s 6d per year to light.

Stansted railway station in 1916, with staff posing beneath the iron footbridge as an approaching Cambridge-bound locomotive comes round the bend. Sadly this eye-pleasing structure was replaced by a modern concrete bridge when electrification of the line took place in the 1980s. In 1990 the station was renamed Stansted Mountfitchet to avoid confusion with Stansted Airport, thus ending a campaign first started by Mr Green nearly a hundred years ago.

Locals gather as bands lead troops of the Coldstream Guards, Royal Scots Greys and others into Station Road and the railway station forecourt in 1937 during military manoeuvres. Elms Farm Grade 'A' milk is advertised (7d a pint). The premises with the AA sign belong to Mayhew Bros, while next door is A.J. Torey's grocery with perhaps Mrs Torey standing in the doorway.

Craig House School in Park Road. Not much is known of this school but an advertisement in 1906 shows that the principals were the Misses Smith and that it was a school for girls where boarders received every home comfort and preparation for the usual examinations.

Church Road with the original road line and Manor House on the right, *c*. 1907. The diversion of Church Road to its present line took place in around 1867 and was later reported to have added 370 steps to the east door of the church. Until 1923 weddings and funerals had some right to use the old way.

The Almshouses in Church Road, *c*. 1913. These houses were built in 1883 by J.L. Glasscock & Son on a site given by Willam Fuller Maitland. The original ones moved from Hoxton, apparently to make use of the better air. Externally the building is unchanged but internally it has been much modernized in recent years.

Stansted Hall Lodge, Church Road, c. 1911. Note the impressive arch and iron gates that protected and gave restricted carriage and foot entrance via the long, well tended back drive to Stansted Hall.

Stansted Hall standing in the extensive grounds of Stansted Park in c. 1905. At this time the hall was the family home of William Fuller Maitland. The lake (locally known as Black Pond) adds an impressive and tranquil foreground. The site of the former hall is somewhere between this and the church. Many local organizations benefited from his personal interest and generosity.

Queen Victoria's Golden Jubilee in 1887 was the occasion of a great event in the grounds of Stansted Hall on 21 June. The Organizing Committee is pictured here. From left to right, back row: Joshua Green, William Spencer, Henry Trigg Jnr, M.F. Freelove, Charles Hicks. Front row: J. Caygill, Thomas Hicks, Harford Green, Charles Spencer, Henry Trigg Snr, Edward Spencer, Alfred Hicks.

The band at the Jubilee celebrations in 1887.

QUEEN'S JUBILEE, 1887.

PROGRAMME OF SPORTS,

STANSTED PARK,

COMMENCING AT 3 P.M.

	1st Prize.	2nd Prize.
3.0 —100yds. Race, for Youths under 16	Hat	Tie
3.10 —150yds. Hurdle Race, over 16 and under 20	Spade	Fork
3.20 —150yds. Hurdle Race, over 20 and under 30	Scythe	Fork
3.30 —100yds. Flat Race, over 30 and under 40	Scythe	Fork
3.40 —100yds. Flat Race, over 40 and under 50	Bill	Shovel
3.50 —100yds. Sack Race, under 20	Shovel	Fork
4.0 —Three legged Race (100yds.), over 20 and under 40	Forks	Forks
4.10 —Donkey Race (Quarter Mile), First Donkey to win	Hat	Tie
4.20 —150yds. Race, for Youths under 16	Hat	Tie
4.30 —300yds. Race, over 16 and under 20	Spade	Fork
4.40 —300yds. Race, over 20 and under 30	Scythe	Shovel
4.50 —150yds. Hurdle Race, over 30 and under 40	Bill	Fork
5.0 —150yds. Race, over 40 and under 50	Bill	Shovel
5.10 —100yds. Race, over 60 and under 70	Spade	Fork
5.20 —Quarter Mile Race, over 18 and under 20	Hat	Tie
5.30 —Quarter Mile Race, over 20 and under 30	Scythe	Shovel
5.40 —Donkey Race (Quarter Mile), last to win	Hat	Tie
(Owners not to ride own Donkey).		
6.0 —Sack Race, 50yds., over 20 and under 40	Shovel	Fork
6.15 —Wheelbarrow Race (100yds.), over 20 and under 40	Scythe	Spade
6.30 —Wheelbarrow Race (100yds.), over 40 and under 50	Scythe	Spade
6.40 —Women's Race (50yds.), over 50	1lb. Tea	½lb. Tea
6.50 —Tug of War (6 a side), Bentfield St. against Burton End	6s.	
7.0 —Tug of War (6 a side), Stansted st. against Stansted Chappell	6s.	
7.15 —Walking Race (Quarter Mile), under 30	Bill	Spade
7.30 —Obstacle Race (200yds.), under 20	Hat	Tie
7.40 —Three legged Race (100yds.), under 20	Hats	Hats
7.50 —Obstacle Race (200yds.), over 20 and under 40	Shovel	Fork
8.0 —Tug of War between the Victors of preceding Contests	Shovels or Forks	
8.— Walking Race (Quarter Mile), over 30	Spade	Fork
8.10 —Egg and Spoon Race (100yds.), Women over 20 & under 30	Flannel	1lb. Tea

SOME TIME DURING PROGRAMME,

CLIMBING GREASY POLE. Prizes—2 LEGS OF MUTTON.

The sports programme. Note that the prizes of spades, forks, hats and ties were very appropriate for a rural community, most of whose members worked on the land. For women, the prize of tea suggests this was still a luxury item at this time.

QUEEN'S JUBILEE, STANSTED, 1887.

PROGRAMME OF MUSIC.

PART I.

"GOD SAVE THE QUEEN."

1.	March	"Jubilee"	F. Lancaster.
2.	Quadrille	"Battle of Austerlitz"	Belger.
3.	Valse	"Flower of the Field"	Tallott.
4.	Selection	"Reminiscences of England"	J. Hartmann.
5.	Schottische	"Clotilde"	E. Marie.
6.	Polka	"Little Pet"	Smith.
7.	Euphonium Solo	"Village Blacksmith"	
	(Arranged by F. Lancaster), by Sergeant Brown.		
8.	Quadrille	"Comedians"	E. Newton.
9.	Fantasia	"Rose D'Amour"	Belger.
10.	Waltz	"Fantine"	Batiforte.
11.	Polka	"Summer Flowers"	Seaman.
12.	Cornet Solo	"I dream'd a dream"	E. Cook.
	By F. Lancaster.		
13.	Selection	"Irish Airs"	J. Hartmann.
14.	Polka	"Pretty Foot"	L. C. Desormes.
15.	Quadrille	"Inspiration"	Smith.

PART II.

16.	Waltz	"Autumn Blossom"	Harris.
17.	Schottische	"Florrie"	M. Seaman.
18.	Selection	"Reminiscences of Scotland"	E. Newton.
19.	Quadrille	"Joyous Friends"	Smith.
20.	Jubilee Glee	"Hail Victoria"	F. Lancaster.
21.	Valse	"Mia Cara"	P. Bucalossi.
22.	Quadrille	"Old Ireland"	Metcalfe.
23.	Schottische	"Dora"	Smith.
24.	Polka	"Little Treasure"	Smith.
25.	Lancers	"Rip Van Winkle"	C. D'Albert.
26.	Valse	"Cordelia"	Smith.
27.	Selection	"Reminiscences of Wales"	E. Hare.
28.	Quadrille	"Patience"	C. D'Albert.
29.	Galop	"Night Bell"	Lamont.
	(Arranged by F. Lancaster).		

"GOD SAVE THE QUEEN."

Bandmaster ... ... F. A. LANCASTER.

Marlon Bros. Printers, Bishop's Stortford.

The music programme, very little of which would be familiar to music lovers today.

Two views of the grounds of Stansted Hall during the 1887 Jubilee celebrations.

The Arthur Findlay College
Stansted

THE LOUNGE

THE LIBRARY

THE LOWER GALLERY

Between 1923 and 1964, Stansted Hall became the home of the Findlay family. By 1968, when this card was sent, the Hall had become the Arthur Findlay College, the leading spiritualist centre in the country.

Stansted House, *c.* 1920. At this time, the house was home to Sir Thomas and Lady Jackson, followed by Lord and Lady Fitzgerald. Mrs Brown, a local resident, still recalls many a thick fog in which she had to negotiate the long, pitch-black, wooded back drive used by the servants. On one occasion she ended up lost in the brambles, and then received a reprimand for being late with no mention made of damage to clothes or to her person.

St Mary's church in 1907. The church was built around 1120-24 though only the chancel arch and north and south doorways now remain. It was extended in the thirteenth and fourteenth centuries by Sir Roger de Lancaster and his son Sir John and restored in 1829 and in 1888.

The new Stansted Secondary Modern School bordering Forest Hall and Church Road was built to replace the old school on Chapel Hill and opened for lessons in 1962. Beyond the School are sports and playing fields which prior to 1921 were home to Stansted Cricket Club, the pavilion standing somewhere near the background tree on the left.

CHAPEL HILL, STANSTED, ESSEX,

Oct 8th 1901

Mr Arnold Stansted

Dr. to W. ROBINSON,
BUILDER AND UNDERTAKER.

ESTIMATES GIVEN FOR ALL KINDS OF REPAIRS.

1901
Sept   Funeral for the late Miss Arnold

Polished Coffin molded with Brass
furniture finny sidesheet &c
2 Morning Coache & Hearse &
4 Bearers & Refreshment &c &
Church fees for same   £ 9 2 6
                            9 2 6

Settled 10th 1901
W Robinson
With thanks

W. Robinson's funeral bill from 1901.

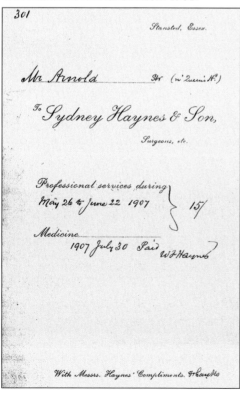

301
                        Stansted, Essex.

Mr Arnold   Dr (to Queen St.)

To Sydney Haynes & Son,
                Surgeons, etc.

Professional services during
May 26 to June 22 1907   } 15/

Medicine
    1907 July 30 Paid WHHaynes

With Messrs. Haynes' Compliments. WHaynes

A doctor's bill from 1907 in pre-NHS days.

Two
Stoney Common and Birchanger

Rochford's Nurseries was established in Stoney Common until its closure in 1970. Some twenty-two acres were covered in glass and around 293 greenhouses had to be heated, just some of which are shown in this view.

Workers in one of the greenhouses, *c.* 1915. In 1927, thirteen acres were devoted to tomatoes and seven acres to Alicante and Muscat grapes for the Cunard liners of the time. Other nursery produce included cucumbers and chrysanthemums.

Tomatoes being loaded onto a truck in Rochford's sidings to convey them to London, *c.* 1925.

Picking tomatoes (above) and cucumbers (below) at Rochford's Nurseries.

Horse transport was used before mechanization came to the nursery.

The Mission Hall was built in 1910 and Sunday services for residents of Stoney Common were conducted by the vicar of Birchanger in whose parish the common lies.

A group of Stoney Common residents outside the Mission Hall. Captain Stevens is in the centre of the front row.

Heard's the grocers at the corner of West Road. The ladies are in the doorway leading to the communal bath house – the cottages had no bathrooms.

The cottages at Stoney Common were built for the workers of Rochford's Nurseries. A gardening magazine *Monthly Pictorial* states in its February 1927 issue: 'There is a small "Port Sunlight" of some sixty cottages, a recreation room, allotments etc. for the benefit of the employees at the nurseries.' In this 1917 view the writer complains of walking alone, 'not with a chap, none to be found here.' The lady delivering bread is further evidence of just how few young men were left in such villages as the demands of war increased.

The workers of Rochford's Nurseries pose beneath a foreman's house, with a water tank as a roof, in the 1890s.

A group of workers in the nursery.

Birchanger church, 1907. Some residents used this as their local church rather than St Mary's or St John's in Stansted.

Birchanger, *c.* 1909.

Birchanger Wood, which still largely exists today though development plans are regularly aired which seem to pose a threat to it.

Three
Bentfield End

In August 1940, Bentfield Hall Hotel, which stood on the corner opposite the fountain and Green's Stores, was almost completely destroyed by fire, despite the best efforts of the Stansted fire brigade who attended with their Morris Commercial tender.

Elizabethan Cottage, Bentfield Causeway, with the family group posing for the camera in 1908. The cottage is still recognizable today. The population of the hamlet of Bentfield at this time was slightly more than 600 people.

Bentfield Place with its well tended conservatory and gardens, possibly occupied at this time by the Gosling family. The grounds and gardens made a lovely setting for the many garden shows and fêtes held there.

Looking north along Bentfield Road in around 1914, with the ivy-covered Eden Cottage (since demolished to make way for modern houses) standing back from the road. The group of workmen are possibly from the Hargrave Estate, as they stand in the rear entrance to Hargrave House.

Lower Bentfield Causeway around 1969, just prior to the days when parking became a problem.

BENTFIELD GREEN, STANSTEAD

Bentfield Green around 1914, with residents outside the Rose and Crown. Albert Welford was the landlord at this time and was noted for his warm welcome to his patrons, a tradition which continues today at all of Stansted's public houses. The field behind the stone wall was the venue for fairground and circus visits on many occasions.

Bentfield Pond, c. 1912. The cottages on the right were probably occupied by the Snow and Woods families. This spot is a perennial favourite with children for feeding the ducks. The writer of the card, a soldier, says that he has marched forty-six miles in two days from Luton.

Berfeld Nook, Stansted.

The 'Nook' stands on the outskirts of Bentfield at the junction with Lime Kiln Lane en route to Manuden. The card was sent by the Nicholson family in 1907.

THE OLD WATER MILL STANSTED

The old water mill at Bentfield, c. 1905. The mill overlooked the millpond and race, which for many years took water from the Stort and nearby springs. The lady posing with her 'high stepper' obviously required great bicycling skill to avoid her long frock becoming entangled with the machine.

Bower Road. Stansted

92

Houses atop Bower Road in 1928 on its sharply twisting way towards Manuden. The writer of the card is on convalescence as were many writers of local cards, so clearly the area was a favourite place for rest and recuperation at the time.

Four
Farnham, Hazel End and Manuden

Farnham Green, *c.* 1908. This is still recognizable today, though hedges prevent the same shot being taken. It is reputed that there used to be a gibbet just off to the left of the picture. In more recent times, maps show that a windmill stood here.

Farnham.

A multi-view card of Farnham, *c.* 1910. Very few postcards of Farnham exist as it is still to this day a very small village. This shows the set of cards that were probably one of the first to be produced. The name was formerly spelt Fernham (Pherneham in Domesday) and gets its derivation from the fern which grew there in large quantities.

Flint Cottages on the road to Manuden, *c.* 1910. Built as estate workers' cottages, they are still recognizable today, though the high banked lanes which are a feature of this area make viewing difficult.

Hassobury, *c.* 1910. Built by the Gosling family between 1868 and 1870, it was used as a convalescent hospital for injured servicemen between 1940 and 1946. In 1976 it became home to Waterside School, which had started life in Bishop's Stortford in 1921, until its closure in 1994.

The pond at Hazel End, 1907. Just out of view is the orchard part of which was given as a burial ground by the Independent Church in Stansted. A number of these burials from 1711 to 1761 are entered in the Farnham parish registers.

Manuden, *c.* 1910. Few guidebooks cover this village, but those that do consider that the wide main street, well kept houses and cottages, thatched roofs and overhanging storeys are worth a stop.

Manuden from the gravel pits, *c*. 1906. The gravel pits no longer exist.

Manuden post office, *c*. 1915.

Another group of charming cottages in The Street, Manuden, *c*. 1915.

Taylor's blacksmith's shop. The date is unknown but is believed to be pre-First World War.

Five

Rickling Green and Quendon

The Coach and Horses, Quendon, *c.* 1905. Quendon stands on the old A11, the main coaching route to Newmarket, and was well supplied with coaching inns. This pretty and most hospitable of inns has recently closed its doors as have several others on this stretch of road over the years.

Rickling Green, *c.* 1906. This is just set back from the A11 and maintains its own centre around the Green.

Quendon church, 1909.

Quendon Hall, seen here *c.* 1905, stands to the north of the village in its own park. Recent owners have included Roger Whittaker, the singer, and Robert Smith, the showjumper and son of Harvey Smith.

Cambridge Road, Quendon, with Mr Cayte in his cart, *c.* 1905. This is the same Mr Cayte that was watering his horse at the fountain in Stansted earlier in this book.

Cambridge Road, Quendon, 1906. This gives some idea of the conditions of this main trunk road before it was covered in tarmac. One can only wonder just how muddy it got in heavy rain.

London Road, Quendon. It is not until 1678 that a map shows Quendon and Stansted to be linked. Before that the road leading to the right went to London via Rickling, the Hadhams and Hoddesdon.

The Street, Quendon, in 1906, with two girls posing outside their house.

Quendon post office, *c.* 1906.

The Pump and Manor House in the 1950s.

The Pump, 1904. At this time, it seems that photographers of village scenes in north-western Essex felt that the presence of a horse and cart was mandatory! It certainly adds interest to the photograph.

The Stores, Quendon, 1920s. These stores are still extant today and feature craft work of all types.

Rickling School, 1911. A typical building for a small village school, which has been extended over the years. Judging from the number of pupils outside, the school roll is now much larger.

The pond at Rickling, *c*. 1905.

Rickling Green, 1913. The houses in this photo were used to board land girls during the Second World War but apart from the cottage on the right they have since been demolished.

Six
Ugley and Ugley Green

The Square, Oakley, 1907. Once the main centre for the village, with shop, post office and inn, it is now a small group of private houses alongside the old A11. At this stage the name of the village had been changed, though the writer of this card underlines Ugley as her address.

The post office, Ugley, 1911. By this time, the village had reverted to its original name. A curious feature is that Lloyds List is advertised, which for an inland rural district seems rather odd.

The White Hart, 1913. This is another of the coaching inns on the A11 that has now become a private house.

Pound Lane, Ugley, 1906. The lane is so named after the village cattle pound where cattle which strayed onto the roads were placed. The farmer could only retrieve these after paying a fine.

Cambridge Road, Ugley, in the 1920s.

Dellows Lane, Ugley, c. 1906. Misspelt by the photographer, this has always been a little lane that meanders along the village, though in the early part of the century it had an off licence and a post office following the closure of the office in the Cambridge Road.

Chestnut Cottage, Ugley, the home of the Dix family, c. 1906.

Ugley Green, showing the school, 1906. Built in 1848, and extended in 1900, the school at one time had a roll of ninety. It closed in 1948, but the buildings remain as private residences.

Vicarage Lane, Ugley, c. 1906. At one time a cottage in this lane was a maltings which sold beer to the local inns.

Fieldgate Farm, Ugley, 1907. This was a turkey farm, though rearing turkeys was very different from today's practice. In *The Ugley Book*, a villager recalls his childhood in the 1920s, when he would gather eggs from turkeys' nests around the fields and hedgerows so that they could be incubated.

The White Cottage, 1909. This cottage was once cut in two and transported by the village doctor to its current position. A villager recalls the time in 1939 when the thatch on the cottage caught fire and another occasion when its photograph appeared in the *Evening Standard* with the caption 'The village that belies its name'.

Orford House 1909. It was built in the late seventeenth century by a distinguished naval officer, Admiral Edward Russell, later Baron Shingay, Viscount Barfleur and Earl of Orford. The Tennant family lived there and were benefactors to the village. The house now belongs to the Home Farm Trust and is home to a number of adults with special needs.

Ugley Hall, *c.* 1906. This was the home of the Robinson family.

The Chequers, Ugley, 1911. The second pub in the village, noted at this time for its dominoes evenings.

The Chequers in the 1950s.

Seven

Elsenham and Henham

OUR LOCAL EXPRESS
from Thaxted to Elsenham
(In the future)

On this 1912 card the Elsenham and Thaxted Light Railway is the butt of the humour of the celebrated Scottish caricaturist Cynicus. Approval for the line was given in 1911 and it was opened by Sir Walter Gilbey on 31 March 1913. Financed partly by the local gentry, it served an area with a traffic potential of less than 3,000 passengers but in its early years it helped to lift the agricultural depression of north-western Essex. The last passenger service ran on 13 September 1952 and the freight service ceased on 1 June 1953.

Elsenham School, *c.* 1910. The school was built in 1863 and extended in 1895 and again in 1902.

The seventeenth-century Crown Inn at Elsenham, *c.* 1912. The landlord from 1909 to 1923 was Charlie Gray and he stands in the doorway. The horse chestnuts have long since gone.

The village pump, 1906. The canopy was erected by Sir Walter Gilbey in memory of his wife who died in 1896. The pump was dismantled in 1958. Behind the pump is the post office, which has long since moved elsewhere in the village.

The High Street, Elsenham, in 1956. The buildings on the left were demolished some years ago.

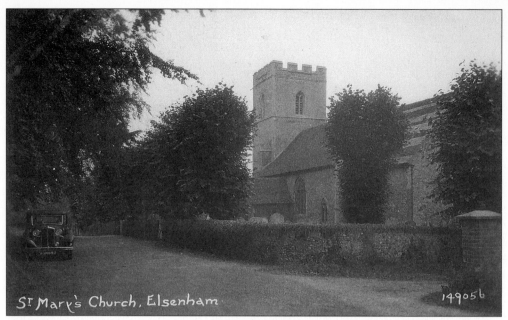

St Mary's, Elsenham, in the late 1920s. The church dates from early in the twelfth century.

Elsenham station (on the Liverpool Street to Cambridge line) with Gold's Nurseries visible on the left, in the late 1930s. The nurseries have gone but the station is still much the same and the level crossing is still hand-operated.

Robin Hood Road with the pub of the same name in the late 1920s or early 1930s. The landlord at the time was Harry Thomas and his Model T Ford is outside. The pub ceased trading about ten years ago and the building was converted into offices.

Fuller's End in 1914, showing cottages from the Estate. Just out of shot is the railway line; the crossing is now closed to motor traffic.

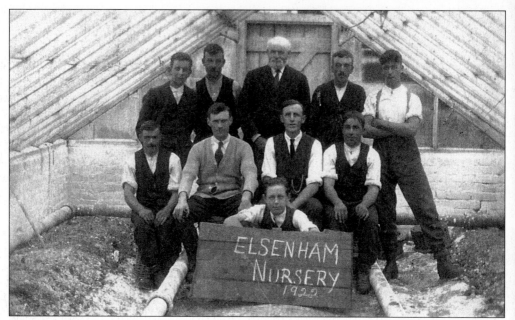

Elsenham Nursery, 1922.

Handpost, 1919. A few years later this was replaced by the War Memorial.

HENHAM

Henham in 1996. A recent multi-view of scenes from the village.

Sheepcote Lane, c. 1908. This was a quiet green lane which an older resident recalls was beloved by courting couples.

A Christmas card sent in 1908 by the Glazebrooks, with the address shown as Wood Farm, Henham, Stansted. It is in fact Pledgdon Green outside Henham.

The thirteenth-century Henham church of St Mary in 1920. In the churchyard is an iron covering built over a grave, a relic from the early days of medicine when dead bodies were frequently taken for anatomical research.

Henham in 1913. This was the era when cycling was in fashion and similar cards may be found from villages all over north-western Essex.

A May Day celebration in 1907 as published in *This England* magazine. Despite the text, the event took place in Henham and Glebe Cottage may be seen in the background.

Eight

Around Stansted Airport

Stansted Airport was built in 1942-43 by the Americans and was operational until August 1945 when the airfield was handed over to the RAF. This shows the construction of a hangar with B26 Marauder bombers in the background.

Manoeuvring heavy airport construction equipment through narrow country lanes and village streets was never easy as this contemporary photograph shows. Here equipment is being transported from the railway sidings, with the hairpin corner of Church Road and Lower Street to negotiate immediately ahead. The railway bridge was specially strengthened to accommodate such loads.

B26 bomber *Sad Sack* of 344 Bomb Group being refuelled prior to a bombing mission.

With the departure of the USAF and later the RAF, the airfield opened for civilian use on 14 December 1946. However, the Americans returned between 1954 and 1957 and extended the runway to 10,000ft, at the time the longest runway in Britain, to handle the B52 bombers. In 1966 BAA took control. After various White Papers and lengthy public inquiries the airfield was declared London's third airport in June 1985. This 1980s card shows aircraft operating from Stansted at the time.

Four views of Stansted Airport before the new terminal was built. At this time the airport was little used by comparison with today, and everything from the welcoming tulips to the sparsely populated terminal and restaurant made this a pleasurable place to fly from. Part of this older terminal complex is now used for business aviation.

During the weekend of 5/6 June 1983, Stansted Airport played host to a unique visitor, the United States Space Shuttle *Enterprise*, transported piggy-back style upon a specially adapted Boeing 747 aircraft. The event caused considerable chaos on the main roads leading to the airport.

The duo make a spectacular departure home from Stansted. The weekend visit was witnessed by an estimated 250,000 people.

The first part of the dome of the roof of the new terminal being lifted into position as a trial. Subsequently, the new terminal building received much praise from travellers and admirers of modern architecture.

Burton End, *c.* 1908. Although this idyllic, scenic rural view has hardly changed, Stansted Airport now lies beyond the cottages and the M11 in a cutting behind the trees.

The Ash, Burton End, *c.* 1948. This popular thatched public house overlooks the west side of the airfield, and introduced many American service personnel to the delights of English ales. Although modernized and extended, it is well remembered by those that have revisited their old station, and a selection of photographs of those days grace the walls.

Tye Green, 1916. Pimblett's Cottage in the small hamlet just outside Elsenham, between Burton End and Fullers End, now directly overlooks Stansted Airport.

The post office, *c.* 1915. This has had several changes of use since that time.

Takeley Street, *c*. 1911. It straggles along the A120, with buildings mostly on the northern side of the road. The A120, the Roman Road known as Stane Street, runs along the northern edge of Hatfield Forest. The 1,000 acres is one of the last remaining royal forests.

Four Ashes crossroads, 1950s. Even as recently as this, traffic lights were not necessary to control the traffic.

Speller's shop, *c.* 1910.

The Chestnuts, *c.* 1956. This was formerly the post office and is now business premises.

Warish Hall, 1905.

The Vicarage, Takeley.

The vicarage at Takeley, c. 1916.

Four Ashes, *c.* 1911. This pub is at the crossroads, the right-hand branch of which now leads to Stansted Airport. The traffic queues here during peak times are quite horrendous and it is difficult to believe that this was such a quiet spot.

Takeley Street, 1916.

Molehill Green in 1906, now a small hamlet on the edge of the airport. Still a quiet spot, it enjoys spectacular views of aircraft landing or taking off from the airport, and the pub and the roads nearby are beloved by aircraft spotters.

Molehill Green in 1935.

Nine

Sports, Leisure and Local Organizations

A splendid shot of the finish of a Bishop's Stortford A & BC cycle race in 1906, which according to the original owner was taken in the Stansted area though the precise location is unknown. It could be on the old A11, which is still the scene of such races today.

A 1904 view of Stansted golf links with the village in the background. The nine-hole course was laid out in 1902 by Aveston of Cromer with G. Harvey as the club professional and extended from the Castle Hills towards the railway and Elsenham. It opened in January 1903 (in the opinion of a leading professional 'It will make a course of no mean order') but closed at the beginning of the First World War. A replica of the Norman castle which formerly stood on the site has now been built and has become a tourist attraction.

The Golf House overlooking the green was thought to have been constructed soon after the course opened. On Whit Monday 1903 a bogey competition was held where the Stansted ladies beat Harlow. The annual membership subscription was two guineas. An old golf ball found during recent river diversions was dated to this playing period and is now at the Bishops Stortford Golf Club. The club house is now a private residence.

This is believed to be the golf club committee. The date and the names are unknown though it clearly dates to before the First World War.

Competitive football matches were being played at Stansted by 1891. The successful team of the 1930s is still remembered by older residents. Here is the victorious Stansted Football Club following their successful 1934/35 season, from left to right, back row: B. Ingold, J. Speller, ? Harling, F. Turner (keeper), F. Wooten, P. Bayford, L. Law, ? Wright, F. Wells. Front row: H. Gray, J. Frost, E. Cawkell, E. Haggerwood, ? Harvey, K. Little, P. Heal.

Stansted FC in 1924/25, at Green's Meadow (where the twelve houses of Greenfields stand today), their home ground until around 1935. The team are standing in front of the Hermitage which was used for changing and other club purposes. It still stands in the front garden of a modern house on Chapel Hill. The war years of 1914-18 saw many players being called for active service and it was not until the 1919/20 season that the side was fully established again as Stansted Rovers.

A bowling green was prepared in a pretty corner of Green Meadow for the Stansted Bowling Club and was formally opened for play on 1 June 1910 when the president, William Fuller Maitland, bowled the jack and took part in the first game. It is thought that this photograph shows the president, members and guests on the opening day.

Records show that cricket matches were being played in Stansted by 1866 and probably for some long time before then. The Tradesmen versus Working Men was one such fixture, played reportedly upon a very uneven field adjacent to the Castle Hills, this being the reason for the low scoring! The 'Veterans XI' shown here played several fixtures during the war years for the Red Cross and other charitable causes. One such match recorded a cumulative age of 1,540 years for the players!

The 1st X1 in 1923.

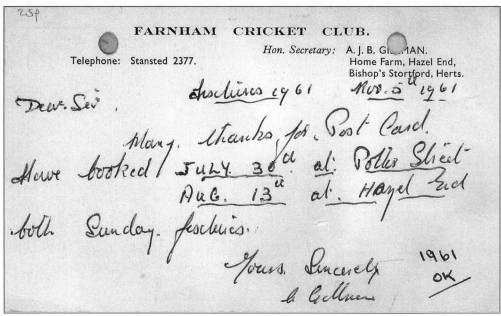

Farnham Cricket Club, 1961. Many cricket club secretaries will recognize such a card, used to confirm agreed fixtures.

Watching the cricket at Rickling Green in the 1950s. This ground is well known in the county and hosts a benefit match each year for the Essex CC player concerned.

Stansted Civil Defence gave invaluable service to the village and surrounding areas during the war years. This photograph is thought to have been taken in the grounds of Crown Cottage and Limes stables. Most names are known: F. Bradford, ? Tabor, R. Waterman, W. Bedlow, P. Smith, W. Turner, ? White, H. Robinson, I. Robinson, ? Carter, J. Watson, J. Mumford, V. Turner, T. Levey, E. Roberts, E. Hanscome, -?-, L. Powell, L. Ridgwell, -?-, ? Brown, -?-, W. Bush, ? Catton, H. Bradford.

Stansted fire brigade stand at ease at Bentfield Hall in 1926 in their new uniforms. Prior to this the only protective clothing was a cap supplied in around 1913 to distinguish firemen from other willing helpers at fires. The engine is a 1914 Shand Mason manual which was to give valiant service for many years. From left to right: A.J. Stockman, B.F. Robinson, L. Smith, H.D. Robinson, A. Nash (Messenger), E. Cawkell (Chief Officer), W.G. Ratcliff (Second Officer), J. Reeves, A. Peachey, L. Powell, W. Mayhew.

Robert Baden-Powell formed the Scouting movement in 1907/08 and Stansted had its own troop by late 1910. This 1911 picture was taken in front of Blythwood Dairy; the names are recorded below. Scouting activities of the time included signalling, knotting and splicing under the instruction of Mr Jobe. In August 1912 Stansted Scouts attended the first Scout Camp at Shackfield going by train to Liverpool Street, then marching through London to Waterloo Station to catch the onward train.

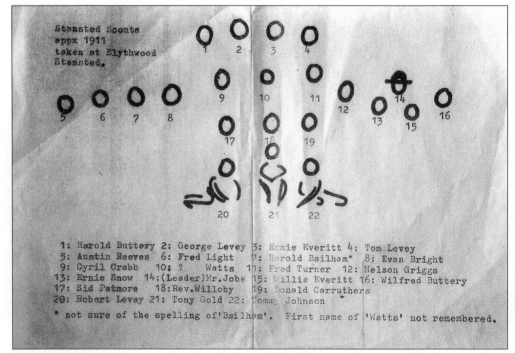

Stansted Scouts
appx 1911
taken at Elythwood
Stansted.

1: Harold Buttery 2: George Levey 3: Ernie Everitt 4: Tom Levey
5: Austin Reeves 6: Fred Light 7: Harold Bailham* 8: Evan Bright
9: Cyril Crabb 10: ? Watts 11: Fred Turner 12: Nelson Griggs
13: Ernie Snow 14:(Leader)Mr.Jobe 15: Willie Everitt 16: Wilfred Buttery
17: Sid Patmore 18:Rev.Willoby 19: Donald Carruthers
20: Robert Levey 21: Tony Gold 22: Tommy Johnson

* not sure of the spelling of 'Bailham'. First name of 'Watts' not remembered.

Boy Scouts and scoutmaster in Ugley in 1915. In all probability these Scouts are off to a weekend camp with their hand cart packed with camping equipment.

An interior view of the Mission Hall, Stoney Common, 1911. An exhibition is in progress, with musical accompaniment by a group including Edward Cawte (with the violin).

Stansted infants' school c. 1905. The teacher is believed to be Miss Woolley. The only known child is Gladys Cawte, fifth from the left in the third row.